"Promise of Eternal Love: Intertwined Destinies"

Synopsis

In a world where time seems to dictate the course of love, Isabella and Elías discover that some bonds cannot be broken, not even by time, distance, or fate. United by a promise made in their youth and separated by circumstances beyond their control, their paths cross again in adulthood, when the wounds of the past still throb strongly.

Through letters never sent, memories that refuse to disappear, and coincidences that seem guided by the universe, both must decide if it is possible to rewrite their story or if eternal love is just a romantic illusion.

A novel where the past and present intertwine in a dance of emotions, decisions, and second chances. Promise of Eternal Love: Intertwined Fates is a story that will make you believe in the power of true love… and in the invisible threads that connect souls destined to find each other.

Table of Contents

Promise of Eternal Love: Intertwined Destinies

Chapter 1: The day everything changed

The summer sun shone brightly over the small town of Valle Sereno. The quiet, cobblestone streets seemed suspended in time, as if nothing bad could happen there. But for Isabella, that day marked the beginning of the end.

She was seventeen years old and had a smile that could brighten even the darkest of days. He, Elías, was an inveterate eighteen-year-old dreamer who loved writing poems in the back of his school notebooks. They met when they were just kids, but it was that particular summer when something changed. When their friendship gave way to something deeper… something neither of them could name at the time.

That July 12th, Isabella ran to the field where they used to meet, a letter in her hands and her heart pounding like a drum. She knew she had to tell him. She knew her life was about to take an unexpected turn, and Elías had to know before it was too late.

When she arrived, he was already there. Sitting under his favorite tree, his eyes closed and his face at peace. As if he'd been waiting for exactly that moment.

"I have to tell you something..." she said, breaking the silence.

He looked at her with that tenderness that had always made her feel the world was a safe place.

—Me too, he replied.

And at that moment, fate decided to intervene.

A black car stopped in the distance. It was her father. He looked at her with cold, impatient eyes. The change she had so feared was materializing before her eyes.

"Isabella, get in the car. We're leaving now," her father ordered in a dry voice.

"Are we going? Where?" Elias asked, confusion etched on his face.

She could only stare at him, her eyes brimming with tears, unable to find the words. She didn't have any. She couldn't say them. She just handed him the letter she'd written for him... and ran to the car.

Elias stood there alone, watching the person he loved most disappear down the road, not knowing if he would ever see her again.

And that's how it all began.

The day everything changed.

Chapter 2: Promises under the sky

Elías didn't return to the countryside for days. The place that had once been his refuge now ached. Every corner of the landscape seemed to bear Isabella's name: the wildflowers she used to pick, the tree trunk where they carved their initials, the immense sky they dreamed of conquering together. Everything was imbued with her.

The letter Isabella had left him was still untouched. He didn't open it right away. He carried it in his jacket pocket, as if by keeping it closed, he could delay the pain he knew it contained.

One night, unable to bear the uncertainty any longer, Elijah climbed the hill where they used to gaze at the stars. The sky was clear, as it had always been when they were together.

He sat down on the grass, feeling the wind on his face, and with trembling hands, he opened the letter.

*"Elijah:

I don't know how to start this. I'm struggling to find the words. Maybe because none of this should be happening. I'm leaving, and I don't know for how long. My father says it's final, but in my heart... I feel it isn't.

This isn't a goodbye, even if it seems like one. It's a promise.

No matter where I am, or how much time passes, I will always love you.

Someday, Elias... when the time is right, our paths will cross again.

Promise me you won't forget me.

Isabella."*

Elias clutched the letter to his chest. Tears streamed down his face, unstoppable. Despite the pain, a spark ignited inside him. A promise had been made that night, under the starry sky they both loved.

And he would fulfill it.

No matter how much time passed.

Chapter 3: Letters without an addressee

The years began to pass, like leaves carried by the wind. Elías clung to his routine, to his studies, to a life that continued to move forward without waiting for anyone. But every evening, upon returning home, he sat at his desk, opened his worn notebook, and wrote to Isabella.

He never knew where to send them. He never received a reply. But writing to her was his way of staying close, of not forgetting her, of keeping alive the promise they both made under that starry sky.

"Isabella, it rained today like when you cried watching sad movies. I thought about you. About how you laughed when I said love could conquer anything. Do you still believe that? Because I do."

"Today was my graduation. I wished you were there. I thought if I closed my eyes tight, I'd see you in the crowd. But you weren't there. And it hurts."

"It's been three years. And yet there isn't a single day that goes by that I don't think of you. I wonder if you receive my letters in your dreams."

Meanwhile, in another city, Isabella was also writing. She did so in the early hours of the morning, when silence weighed more than memories. In her diary, hidden under the mattress, were pages filled with "Elías" written in blue ink and invisible tears.

Her life in the city was very different. Colder, faster, more filled with demands than feelings. Her father had forced her to attend a strict private school, surrounded by people who didn't know her story. Who didn't know about a boy who had promised her eternal love.

"Elias... if only you knew how much I miss you. Sometimes I wake up thinking I'll be back in the country and you'll be there, waiting for me."

"I don't know if you still remember me. But I carry you with me, in every song, in every corner where the sky is as big as your dreams."

Both were writing. Both were waiting. Unaware that fate had already begun to silently pull its strings.

Chapter 4: The Unexpected Farewell

Isabella looked out the classroom window as the teacher talked about mathematical formulas. Her mind, however, was far from that place. It returned, again and again, to the field in Valle Sereno, to the tree where she left Elías, to the last wordless glance they shared.

It was her senior year of high school, and everything around her felt empty. Her father, stricter than ever, had gotten another promotion that meant moving again, this time to another country. The United

States. A "golden" opportunity, according to him. A decision already made. Without consultation. Without warning.

"We're leaving on Friday. Everything's already arranged," he said one evening as they sat eating in silence.

Isabella dropped her fork. Her hands shook, and the air became thicker than she could breathe.

"Again? I'm just getting used to it, Dad..." she whispered, feeling her voice crack.

—It's for your future. You'll have better opportunities there. And besides, it's time you left those fantasies of the past behind.

The phrase was like a slap in the face. "Fantasies of the past." As if Elías and everything they shared were a mere childish illusion.

That night, Isabella cried silently, clutching her diary. It wasn't just a move. It was another goodbye. One that now felt final. Elías was further away than ever, and now he would be even further away.

The next day, she skipped class and went to the train station. She bought a ticket with the little money she had saved. She didn't tell anyone. She couldn't leave without seeing him again. She needed answers. Closure. A real goodbye.

Meanwhile, Elías was working at the town bookstore, his first formal job. He wasn't expecting anything special from that day… until he looked up and saw her walk through the door.

The world stopped.

She was still the same. Maybe taller, with longer hair, but her eyes… her eyes were the same ones that had looked at him that July 12th.

"Isabella…" he said, as if he didn't believe it was real.

She smiled, through tears.

—I came to say goodbye. This time… for real.

Chapter 5: Echoes of the Past

The silence between them was so thick it could be cut with air. They stood face to face, like two strangers recognizing each other in a universe that is no longer the same. And yet… the connection remained, intact, as if time had stopped just for them.

"Why did you leave like that?" Elias asked, his voice barely a whisper.

Isabella looked down. Her hands were shaking, just like that afternoon under the tree.

—I had no choice. My father decided everything. He didn't even let me say goodbye the way I wanted. All I could do was leave you that letter… and walk away.

He nodded, swallowing the anger he'd been building up for years. Not at her, but at the helplessness of not being able to do anything.

—And now? Are you leaving again?

—Yes. This time… it's further. The United States. In two days.

Elias felt something inside him slowly break. He had dreamed of that reunion a thousand times, but never like this. Never so brief. Never with another goodbye on the horizon.

—I never forgot you, Isabella.

She looked at him, her eyes moist.

—Me neither. Every letter you wrote, every word… I wrote them too. Even though I didn't know where you were. Even though I couldn't send them to you.

He was surprised.

—Were you writing to me too?

—Yes. I have notebooks full of you. Of us. As if putting it into words could keep you close.

Then Elias took her hand and led her out of the bookstore, toward the field they'd once shared. The sky was beginning to turn orange, and the shadows of the past lengthened among the trees.

—I want to show you something, he said.

Under that old tree, the same one that had seen them laugh, dream, and part ways, there was now a small wooden box buried among the roots. Elías carefully dug it out and opened it. Inside were all the letters he had written to her over the years.

—I never knew where to send them. But I couldn't stop writing to you. So I kept them here, in case you ever came back.

Isabella took them in her hands, her heart overflowing.

And in that instant, as the wind played with their hair and the sun set behind the hills, they realized that what they felt hadn't died. It had only slept.

The echoes of the past weren't just memories. They were promises that still vibrated in their souls.

Chapter 6: The Reunion

Night fell gently over Valle Sereno. Elías and Isabella walked slowly along the path that led back to the village, holding hands, as if the simple touch could halt the passage of time.

The world seemed to be on pause. All around them was calm and sighing, as if even nature knew that this moment was unique.

"What if you don't leave?" Elias asked suddenly, stopping halfway.

Isabella looked at him, surprised. His face was bathed in the dim moonlight, and for a moment, she wished he wasn't looking at her like that... because she knew she wouldn't be able to resist.

"It's not that simple," she said sadly. "My father... he... he's already got everything planned. And it's not just him. There's also my mother, my studies..."

Elias clenched his jaw. He understood the reasons, but they hurt just the same.

—Then stay alone tonight. One more night… as if nothing had changed. As if time had stopped for us.

She didn't respond with words. She just nodded, tears in her eyes. And so, like two souls seeking refuge, they allowed themselves to be swept away by nostalgia and love.

They went to the old wooden bridge, where they used to play as children. There, amid shy laughter and memories, Elias took a small velvet box out of his pocket. It wasn't a ring or an expensive piece of jewelry. Inside was a simple pendant with a blue stone, the same one Isabella had once said was her favorite color.

—I bought it when you turned eighteen… just in case you ever came back. I never knew if I'd give it to you, but… here it is.

Isabella took the pendant and cherished it as if it were a treasure. Then she hugged it tightly, unwilling to let go.

—Thank you for not forgetting me, he whispered.

—I never could.

That night they slept under the stars, cuddled together, sharing the warmth of their story. There were no promises of the future, no certainties. There was just them, together at last, in the only place they'd always belonged: in each other's arms.

And as they closed their eyes, they knew that love is not measured by how long it lasts, but by how deep it is felt.

Chapter 7: Doubts and silences

Dawn found Isabella and Elías still embracing, wrapped in a blanket lent by the universe. They didn't speak much when they woke up. The silence spoke for them. It was a gentle silence, full of tenderness... but also fear.

The clock ticked more cruelly than ever. Only a few hours remained before Isabella's departure. And although their bodies were close, their thoughts were in opposite corners of uncertainty.

They walked together to the train station, where Isabella was to catch the shuttle that would take her to the airport in the neighboring city. With every step, she felt like a piece of her soul was being ripped out. Elías walked beside her, his hands in his pockets, struggling not to ask her to stay.

"What if this is the last time?" she asked, stopping suddenly.

—It won't be.

The confidence in Elias's voice was firm, but his eyes didn't lie: fear was eating him up inside.

—Tell me you're going to wait for me, Isabella said, with a lump in her throat.

-Always.

He looked into her eyes, unwavering. "But I don't want you to feel tied to a promise. I want you to follow your path, to discover who you are. If one day, fate brings us together again... it will be because it was meant to be."

—And if not?

—Then at least we'll know we tried. That we truly lived it.

Isabella took a deep breath. Her soul was divided into two worlds: the one that demanded she move on, and the one that begged her to stay.

Before he could reply, a message came in on his cell phone. His father: "The flight leaves in three hours. Don't be late."

Reality hit hard. There was no more time.

They embraced one last time, a long, silent, desperate embrace. And when the train arrived, Isabella boarded without looking back. Not because she didn't want to... but because if she did, she wouldn't have the strength to continue.

Elias stood on the platform, watching the train pull away. His fingers still trembled from the fresh warmth of his hand. He felt emptiness in his chest, but also a certainty: it wasn't the end.

It was the beginning of something new. Something they didn't yet understand... but that would continue to unite them, regardless of the distance.

Chapter 8: One Look, a Thousand Memories

Three years later.

Elías had changed. He was no longer the young dreamer who wrote letters under a tree, although deep down, he was still the same. Now he studied literature at university and worked as an editor at a small independent publishing house. His world revolved around books, steaming coffee, and thoughts that still, from time to time, bore Isabella's name.

Every time he saw a blue stone or smelled the wet earth after the rain, his mind brought her back. Not with pain, but with that sweet nostalgia that only true love leaves.

Isabella, for her part, lived in New York. The city had devoured her at first, with its noise, its speed, and its demands. But she had learned to survive. To become resilient. She studied psychology, and

in her free time, she continued to write in her diary… although now
the pages spoke more about her than about him.

Every so often, though, when she saw a couple holding hands or
heard a song about promises, her mind would return to the
countryside, the bridge, the blue pendant she still kept in a box next
to her bed.

One afternoon, Elías walked into an art gallery. His best friend,
Clara, was exhibiting her paintings, and he had promised to
accompany her. He was walking among the works, holding a glass
of wine, when he suddenly stopped.

A picture hanging on the wall took his breath away.

It was a painting of a hill, a starry sky, and a lonely tree. All covered
in an atmosphere of love and farewell. It was her tree. Her sky. Her
story.

"That's my place..." he murmured.

"Do you recognize him?" Clara asked, appearing at his side.

—Who painted it?

—An artist who arrived from New York a few months ago. Her name is Isabella.

Elijah's heart stopped for a second. The wine almost fell from his hands.

—Isabella? Do you have her contact?

Clara looked at him with a smile that said more than he could understand at that moment.

—Maybe you don't need it. Look closely.

Elias looked at the painting again.

And then he saw her.

Across the gallery, Isabella stood in front of another work, staring into space… until she turned around.

Their eyes met.

A look.

And a thousand memories burst between them.

Chapter 9: Untold Secrets

Elías crossed the gallery as if time didn't exist, as if not a single day had passed since that farewell at the station. Isabella, motionless, watched him approach, her heart pounding in her chest as if it wanted to escape from her body.

When they were finally face to face, they said nothing.

It was not necessary.

Their eyes spoke with the power of a thousand letters never sent. With the silences of entire nights longing for an impossible reunion.

"Hello..." she said, breaking the spell.

—Hi, Isa.

That simple nickname brought tears to Isabella's eyes. It had been years since anyone had called her that.

They sat together on a bench inside the gallery, surrounded by paintings and other people's stories, while their own story slowly wove itself between them.

—I didn't think I'd see you again, Isabella said.

—Me neither. Although I always wanted to.

She looked down.

—When I left… I was so afraid of forgetting you. But it was impossible. I carried you with me through everything. In my decisions, in my fears, in my dreams. You were always there.

"And you in me," Elijah replied. "Sometimes I wondered if you were real, or just a promise I made up so I wouldn't lose myself."

Isabella smiled sadly.

—I didn't want to go back without knowing who I was. Without being able to look you in the eyes and tell you that I didn't need you to be strong… but that I still loved you.

There was a silence, one of those that doesn't bother, but rather heals.

"I also have something I didn't tell you," Elias confessed, his voice barely steady. "After you left... a part of me wanted to move on. I had other stories. Or attempts. But I could never love anyone like I loved you."

Isabella looked at him, with a sparkle in her eyes that can only be born from love that survives time.

—I tried too… but no one made my soul tremble like you.

Elias took her hand, slowly, as if he feared that contact would break the magic.

—And now what do we do with all this?

Isabella took a deep breath. For the first time in years, her voice was clear and firm:

—Now we let love hide no more. Not behind letters, nor paintings, nor fear. This time… we live it.

And so, amid secrets finally revealed and truths they had waited too long for, they understood that some promises are never broken. They just sleep, waiting for the right moment to be reborn.

Chapter 10: Intertwined Destinies

Elías and Isabella walked together through the city streets like two teenagers escaping time. They didn't talk much. There was no need to. The glances, the smiles, the subtle touches of their hands spoke volumes their hearts had held for years.

They ended up in a small café, tucked away between brick buildings with flowers in the windows. There, sitting face to face, cups of coffee steaming between them, they began to talk about what was coming up.

"I have a gallery that wants to exhibit my work in Paris," Isabella said, looking out the window with a mixture of excitement and fear.

"It's a huge opportunity. But I'm scared... of having to choose between what I love and who I love again."

Elias nodded. He knew what it meant to her, what she'd fought for to get there.

—You shouldn't have to choose. True love doesn't limit... it accompanies.

Isabella looked at him, and in her gaze there was a silent question: Will you be there if I come?

Elias smiled.

—I can work from anywhere. I'm no longer the boy who clung to a town. I'm a man who learned that if love knocks a second time, you shouldn't let it go.

She took his hand on the table.

—What if this isn't easy either? What if we break up again?

—Then we'll meet again. Because there are promises that don't need to be repeated. They live in the soul.

That night, Isabella took him to her apartment. Not on impulse, but because she felt she'd found her home, not in a place… but in him. For the first time in a long time, there were no fears. Only certainties.

The next morning, they woke up arm in arm, with sunlight streaming through the window and the city roaring below, oblivious to what they had whispered about.

That same week, they bought two tickets to Paris.

Together.

Because this time, their destinies were not only intertwined by love, but also by the decision to never let go again.

Chapter 11: Under the Parisian Sky

Paris welcomed them with soft spring rain and a sky covered in golden clouds. Isabella and Elias walked through the cobblestone streets as if they already belonged to this new world. Everything seemed new to them, yet strangely familiar. As if, somehow, they had already lived that life… in their dreams.

Isabella settled into a small but cozy studio near Montmartre. The white walls were soon filled with blue brushstrokes, sketches, canvases, and that creative energy that only she could summon. Elías, meanwhile, joined a French publishing house that published poetry and foreign literature. On his desk, right next to his laptop, there was always a photo: Isabella laughing under the tree in the countryside, years ago.

Every morning began with hot coffee and soft kisses. Every night ended with books, paintings, and plans for the future. But not everything was perfect.

Paris, with all its art and beauty, also had its shadows.

There were days of doubt, of stress, of unspoken words. Moments when Isabella felt like she was losing her identity amid exhibitions, interviews, and reviews. Days when Elías wondered if she would one day miss the silence of the village more than the city that now surrounded them.

But in each of those doubts, they chose each other.

One night, Isabella returned late from a presentation. She was exhausted, emotionally drained, and upon entering the apartment, she found Elías asleep on the couch with an open book on his chest. She approached him quietly, looked at him tenderly… and cried.

"I don't know if I'm ready for all this," she whispered into the darkness.

"No one is," he replied, waking up without opening his eyes. "But if you're with me, we'll face it together."

That was his simplest and strongest truth.

A few days later, while they were strolling along the Seine, Elias surprised her with an unexpected gesture. He stopped on one of the bridges and, taking the old blue pendant he still had from his pocket, said:

—I never asked you to stay… but now I want to ask you something different.

Isabella looked at him, her heart beating as if she were returning to the first day.

-That?

—Would you stay and build this life with me? Not out of fear of the past… but out of love for the present.

She did not respond with words.

She just hugged him, tightly, as if that promise—finally, finally— would become eternal under the Parisian sky.

Chapter 12: Always You

The years passed, but not love.

Paris had shaped them, taught them how to fall, how to get back up, how to rebuild. And in the process, they had learned the most important thing: true love isn't perfect, it's constant.

Isabella became a renowned artist, with exhibitions in various European cities. Her work always spoke of the soul, of love, and of time. And in every stroke, in every shadow, Elías was always there. Even when he wasn't on the canvases, he was her inspiration.

Elías published his first book, a collection of short stories titled
Letters to Silence, dedicated to "the woman who turned every wait
into poetry." Critics loved it, but he only smiled when he saw
Isabella cry as she read the dedication.

They shared days that felt like eternity. Cooking together. Walking
in the rain. Fighting over trivial matters. Making up with a song.
Watching movies while cuddled up. And yes, they also dreamed of a
future with children, a house by the sea, and more years to love each
other.

One day, sitting in a cafe facing the river, Isabella took Elías's hand
and said:

—Do you know the moment I knew you were the love of my life?

He looked at her, curious.

—When you let me go. You didn't hold me back, you didn't tie me
down. You gave me freedom… and you waited for me
unconditionally. Not just anyone can do that.

—I knew if the love was real, you'd come back.

She smiled, her eyes sparkling.

—It was always you, Elias. In every decision, on every path, in every return… it was always you.

He kissed her with the delicacy of someone who knows that love is fragile, but eternal.

And she understood that the years, the kilometers or the tests didn't matter.

Because when two souls are made to meet, the universe brings them together again and again… until they stay.

Together.

No empty promises.

Only love.

Eternal love.

END

Epilogue: Where it all begins again

Ten years later.

The sea gently lapped the shore in front of a white house with blue windows, surrounded by bougainvillea and children running through the garden. Elías watched from the porch, a cup of coffee in one hand and a notebook in the other. He no longer wrote for relief, but out of gratitude.

Isabella stepped out into the garden wearing a wide-brimmed hat and a bright smile. In her arms, a light-eyed girl played with a blue pendant around her neck—the same one that had once been a promise, then a memory… and now a legacy.

—Dad, tell me how you met Mom again, the girl asked, sitting next to him.

Elias smiled, as if it were the first time.

—It was a magical summer in a town where heaven seemed closer… and where I met the person who would change my life forever.

Isabella joined them, sitting on Elias's lap, while the girl lay on her legs.

—And you went with her?

"She left first," he replied, stroking his daughter's hair, "but fate... fate did its thing. It always does when it comes to true love."

The girl closed her eyes with a smile, already dreaming of her own stories.

Isabella looked at Elias and whispered:

—Thanks for waiting for me.

He kissed her forehead tenderly.

—It would always have been you, Isa. In any life.

The wind blew, carrying with it the murmur of fulfilled promises.

And in that house facing the sea, where the past and the future embraced, love lived on.

Not like a story that ends…

But as a story that, every day, began again.

END OF THE EPILOGUE

Acknowledgments

Thank you for staying with me until the last page of this story.

This book was born from a love of words and a deep belief that destinies, when intertwined by the soul, always meet again.

Thanks to those who have loved, lost, and loved again.

Thanks to my family for their patience.

To the friends who believe in my lyrics.

And to you, reader, for bringing this story to life with your imagination.

Without you, these pages would be meaningless.

About the author

Rumini Peña is passionate about stories that explore human emotions, the bonds of the soul, and the invisible paths forged by destiny. She is the author of novels, reflection books, and personal development books.

Writing is her way of healing, of understanding the world, and of leaving a mark on the hearts of those who read her words.

When she's not writing, she dreams of new stories, gazes at the sky, and believes deeply in life-changing reunions.

Also by the author

If you enjoyed Promise of Eternal Love: Intertwined Destinies, you might be interested in reading other titles by the author:

- Silenced: A Deep Look at Violence Against Women

  Subtitle: The fight against the shadow of violence

- Finding Inner Peace: A Journey Toward Personal Harmony

  Subtitle: A world of personal peace

Different stories, but with the same heart: the desire to touch the reader's soul.

Did you like this story?

If this novel resonated with you, if it made you sigh, cry, or believe in love again…

share it.

Leave a review.

Recommend it.

Your voice helps words continue traveling around the world.

Thanks for reading.

With love,

Rumini Peña